TABLE OF CONTENTS

Colours	3	Feelings	28
Shapes	6	Relatives	30
Numbers 0-10	8	Animals	34
Numbers 11-100	10	Insects	37
Large Numbers	12	Ocean Life	38
Seasons	13	Vehicles	40
Months	14	Sea & Air Transport	43
Days of the Week	15	Fruit	44
Telling the Time	16	Vegetables	46
Weather	20	Food	48
Nature	22	Clothes	50
Solar System	24	Jyutping	51
The Body	25	QR codes	52

For Riley, JJ & Bella
and all other learners

This vocabulary book is written in traditional Chinese with Jyutping pronunciations. It is intended as a pictorial introduction to spoken Cantonese for new learners, or for those wishing to brush up or learn more vocabulary. Alternative spoken forms are included where possible, and the formal written form of the word or phrase is denoted by an (f) in brackets.

Thank you for reading this book. I really hope you like it. It has taken me a long time to produce this and there were many more sections I wanted to include. I would love to get your feedback and can be contacted at littlecantolearning@gmail.com.

All rights reserved. No part of this publication may be reproduced, stored in a retrieval system, or transmitted in any form or by any means, electronic, mechanical, photocopying, recording, or otherwise, without the permission of the copyright owner.

Copyright © Farina Leong 2023
First published January 2023

ISBN: 9781739759629

顏色 COLOURS
ngaan4 sik1

紅色 hung4 sik1 red

橙色 caang2 sik1 orange

黃色 wong4 sik1 yellow

綠色 luk6 sik1 green

藍色 laam4 sik1 blue

紫色 zi2 sik1 purple

粉紅色 fan2 hung4 sik1 pink

啡色 fe1 sik1 brown

咖啡色 gaa3 fe1 sik1
棕色 zung1 sik1 (f)

3

灰色
fui1 sik1
grey

黑色
hak1 sik1
black

白色
baak6 sik1
white

彩色
coi2 sik1
multi-coloured

深
sam1
dark

淺
cin2
light

粉
fan2
pastel

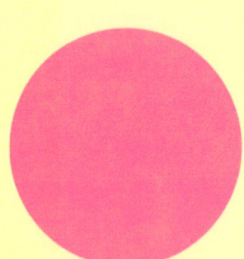
鮮
sin1
bright

金色
gam1 sik1
gold

銀色
ngan4 sik1
silver

古銅色
gu2 tung4 sik1
bronze

鮮紅色
sin1 hung4 sik1
scarlet

橙紅色
caang2 hung4 sik1
orange-red

琥珀色
fu2 paak3 sik1
amber

米色
mai5 sik1
beige

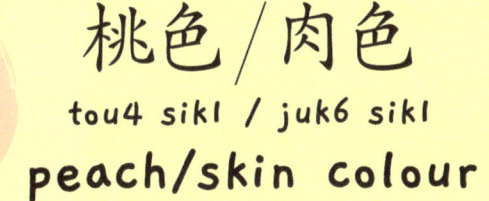
桃色/肉色
tou4 sik1 / juk6 sik1
peach/skin colour

鮮粉紅色
sin1 fan2 hung4 sik1
bright pink

紫紅色
zi2 hung4 sik1
magenta

淺紫色
cin2 zi2 sik1
lilac

橄欖綠
gaam3 laam5 luk6
olive

青綠色
ceng1 luk6 sik1
turquoise

淺藍色
cin2 laam4 sik1
light blue

深藍色
sam1 laam4 sik1
navy blue

靛色
din6 sik1
indigo

形狀 SHAPES
jing4 zong6

圓形
jyun4 jing4
circle

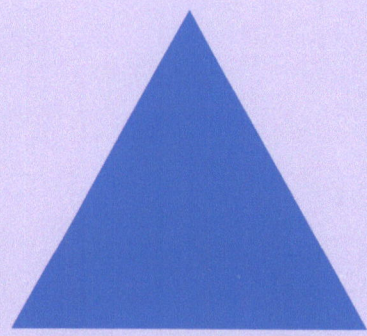

三角形
saam1 gok3 jing4
triangle

正方形
zing3 fong1 jing4
square

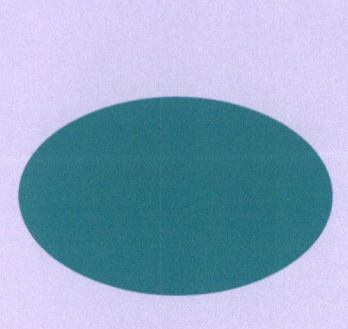

橢圓形
to5 jyun4 jing4
oval

菱形
ling4 jing4
diamond
/rhombus

長方形
coeng4 fong1 jing4
rectangle

心形
sam1 jing4
heart

星形
sing1 jing4
star

梯形
tai1 jing4
trapezoid

五角形
ng5 gok3 jing4
pentagon

六角形
luk6 gok3 jing4
hexagon

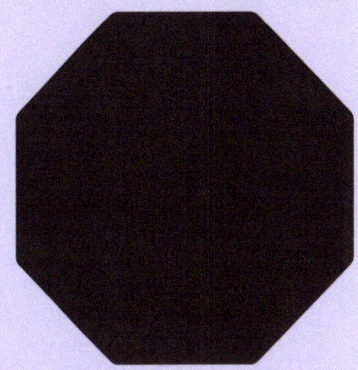

八角形
baat3 gok3 jing4
octagon

數字 sou3 zi6   NUMBERS 0-10

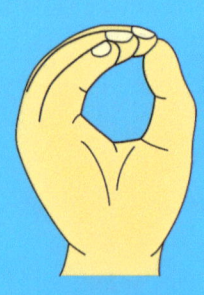
零
ling4
0

一
jat1
1

二
ji6
2

六
luk6
6

七
cat1
7

八
baat3
8

三
saam1
3

四
sei3
4

五
ng5
5

九
gau2
9

十
sap6
10

數字
sou3 zi6

NUMBERS 11-100

十一	十二	十三	十四	十五	十六	十七	十八	十九	二十
11	**12**	**13**	**14**	**15**	**16**	**17**	**18**	**19**	**20**
sap6 jat1	sap6 ji6	sap6 saam1	sap6 sei3	sap6 ng5	sap6 luk6	sap6 cat1	sap6 baat3	sap6 gau2	ji6 sap6

二十一	二十二	二十三	二十四	二十五	二十六	二十七	二十八	二十九	三十
21	**22**	**23**	**24**	**25**	**26**	**27**	**28**	**29**	**30**
ji6 sap6 jat1	ji6 sap6 ji6	ji6 sap6 saam1	ji6 sap6 sei3	ji6 sap6 ng5	ji6 sap6 luk6	ji6 sap6 cat1	ji6 sap6 baat3	ji6 sap6 gau2	saam1 sap6

三十一	三十二	三十三	三十四	三十五	三十六	三十七	三十八	三十九	四十
31	**32**	**33**	**34**	**35**	**36**	**37**	**38**	**39**	**40**
saam1 sap6 jat1	saam1 sap6 ji6	saam1 sap6 saam1	saam1 sap6 sei3	saam1 sap6 ng5	saam1 sap6 luk6	saam1 sap6 cat1	saam1 sap6 baat3	saam1 sap6 gau2	sei3 sap6

四十一	四十二	四十三	四十四	四十五	四十六	四十七	四十八	四十九	五十
41	**42**	**43**	**44**	**45**	**46**	**47**	**48**	**49**	**50**
sei3 sap6 jat1	sei3 sap6 ji6	sei3 sap6 saam1	sei3 sap6 sei3	sei3 sap6 ng5	sei3 sap6 luk6	sei3 sap6 cat1	sei3 sap6 baat3	sei3 sap6 gau2	ng5 sap6

五十一	五十二	五十三	五十四	五十五	五十六	五十七	五十八	五十九	六十
51	52	53	54	55	56	57	58	59	60
ng5 sap6 jat1	ng5 sap6 ji6	ng5 sap6 saam1	ng5 sap6 sei3	ng5 sap6 ng5	ng5 sap6 luk6	ng5 sap6 cat1	ng5 sap6 baat3	ng5 sap6 gau2	luk6 sap6

六十一	六十二	六十三	六十四	六十五	六十六	六十七	六十八	六十九	七十
61	62	63	64	65	66	67	68	69	70
luk6 sap6 jat1	luk6 sap6 ji6	luk6 sap6 saam1	luk6 sap6 sei3	luk6 sap6 ng5	luk6 sap6 luk6	luk6 sap6 cat1	luk6 sap6 baat3	luk6 sap6 gau2	cat1 sap6

七十一	七十二	七十三	七十四	七十五	七十六	七十七	七十八	七十九	八十
71	72	73	74	75	76	77	78	79	80
cat1 sap6 jat1	cat1 sap6 ji6	cat1 sap6 saam1	cat1 sap6 sei3	cat1 sap6 ng5	cat1 sap6 luk6	cat1 sap6 cat1	cat1 sap6 baat3	cat1 sap6 gau2	baat3 sap6

八十一	八十二	八十三	八十四	八十五	八十六	八十七	八十八	八十九	九十
81	82	83	84	85	86	87	88	89	90
baat3 sap6 jat1	baat3 sap6 ji6	baat3 sap6 saam1	baat3 sap6 sei3	baat3 sap6 ng5	baat3 sap6 luk6	baat3 sap6 cat1	baat3 sap6 baat3	baat3 sap6 gau2	gau2 sap6

九十一	九十二	九十三	九十四	九十五	九十六	九十七	九十八	九十九	一百
91	92	93	94	95	96	97	98	99	100
gau2 sap6 jat1	gau2 sap6 ji6	gau2 sap6 saam1	gau2 sap6 sei3	gau2 sap6 ng5	gau2 sap6 luk6	gau2 sap6 cat1	gau2 sap6 baat3	gau2 sap6 gau2	jat1 baak3

大數字 LARGE NUMBERS
daai6 sou3 zi6

一千	jat1 cin1	**1,000** one thousand
一萬	jat1 maan6	**10,000** ten thousand
十萬	sap6 maan6	**100,000** one hundred thousand
一百萬	jat1 baak3 maan6	**1,000,000** one million
一千萬	jat1 cin1 maan6	**10,000,000** ten million
一億	jat1 jik1	**100,000,000** one hundred million

季節   SEASONS
gwai3 zit3

春天
ceon1 tin1
spring

夏天
haa6 tin1
summer

秋天
cau1 tin1
autumn

冬天
dung1 tin1
winter

月份 MONTHS
jyut6 fan6

一月 January jat1 jyut6	二月 February ji6 jyut6
三月 March saam1 jyut6	四月 April sei3 jyut6
五月 May ng5 jyut6	六月 June luk6 jyut6
七月 July cat1 jyut6	八月 August baat3 jyut6
九月 September gau2 jyut6	十月 October sap6 jyut6
十一月 November sap6 jat1 jyut6	十二月 December sap6 ji6 jyut6

星期 DAYS OF THE WEEK
sing1 kei4

星期一 sing1 kei4 jat1 — Monday

星期二 sing1 kei4 ji6 — Tuesday

星期三 sing1 kei4 saam1 — Wednesday

星期四 sing1 kei4 sei3 — Thursday

星期五 sing1 kei4 ng5 — Friday

星期六 sing1 kei4 luk6 — Saturday

星期日 sing1 kei4 jat6 — Sunday

報時 TELLING THE TIME
bou3 si4

一點

jat1 dim2

1 o'clock

兩點

loeng5 dim2

2 o'clock

三點

saam1 dim2

3 o'clock

七點

cat1 dim2

7 o'clock

八點

baat3 dim2

8 o'clock

九點

gau2 dim2

9 o'clock

N.B. You can add 鍾 (zung1), which means 'clock' or 'o'clock' to the end of the time e.g. 一點鍾.

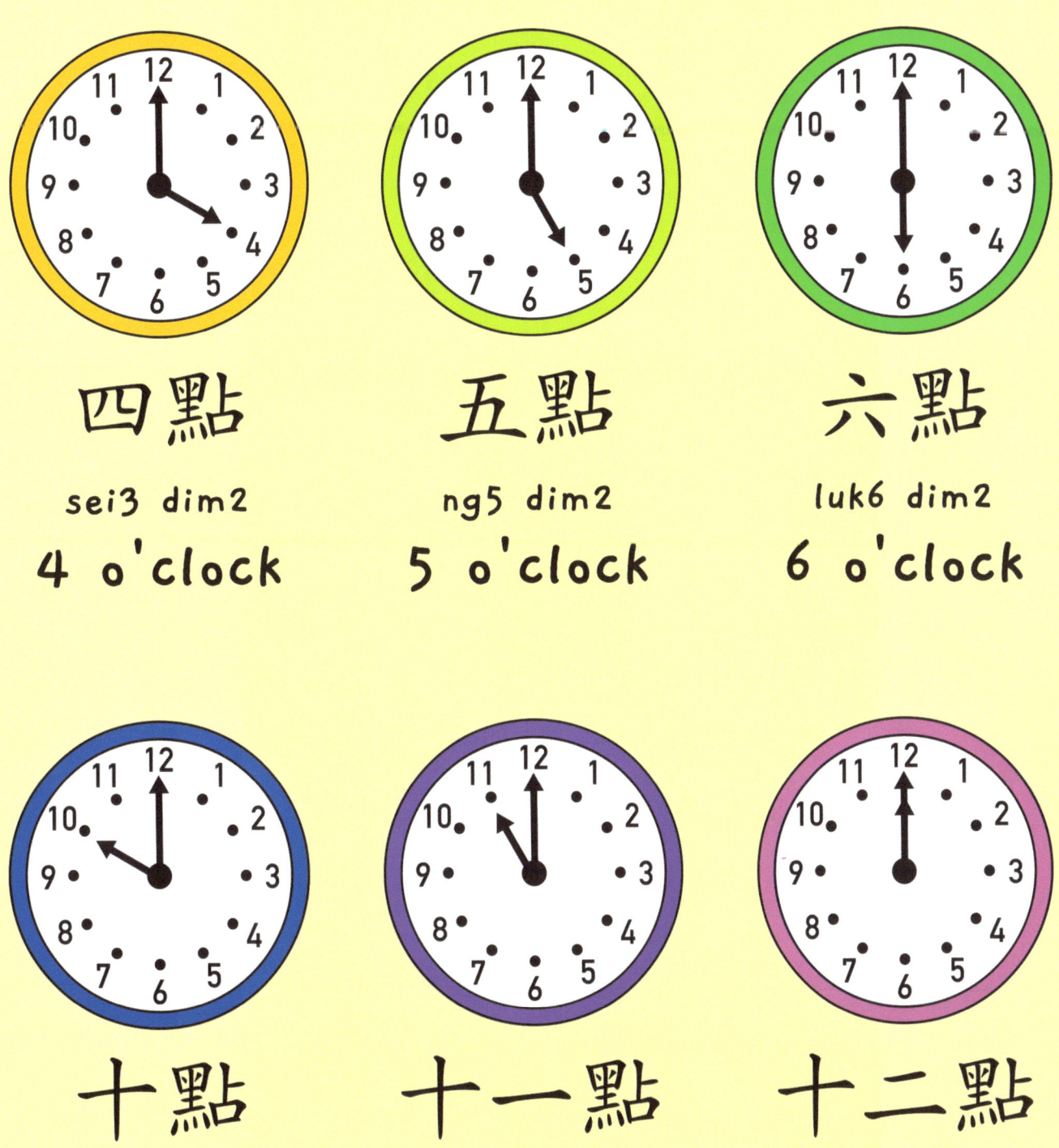

一點一個字
jat1 dim2 jat1 go3 zi6
1.05
一點零五分
jat1 dim2 ling4 ng5 fan1

一點兩個字
jat1 dim2 loeng5 go3 zi6
1.10
一點十分
jat1 dim2 sap6 fan1

一點三個字
jat1 dim2 saam1 go3 zi6
1.15
一點十五分
jat1 dim2 sap6 ng5 fan1

一點七個字
jat1 dim2 cat1 go3 zi6
1.35
一點三十五分
jat1 dim2 saam1 sap6 ng5 fan1

一點八個字
jat1 dim2 baat3 go3 zi6
1.40
一點四十分
jat1 dim2 sei3 sap6 fan1

一點九個字
jat1 dim2 gau2 go3 zi6
1.45
一點四十五分
jat1 dim2 sei3 sap6 ng5 fan1

一點四個字
jat1 dim2 sei3 go3 zi6
1.20
一點二十分
jat1 dim2
ji6 sap6 fan1

一點五個字
jat1 dim2 ng5 go3 zi6
1.25
一點二十五分
jat1 dim2
ji6 sap6 ng5 fan1

一點半
jat1 dim2 bun3
1.30
一點三十分
jat1 dim2
saam1 sap6 fan1

一點十個字
jat1 dim2 sap6 go3 zi6
1.50
一點五十分
jat1 dim2
ng5 sap6 fan1

一點十一個字
jat1 dim2 sap6 jat1 go3 zi6
1.55
一點五十五分
jat1 dim2
ng5 sap6 ng5 fan1

天氣 WEATHER
tin1 hei3

太陽
taai3 joeng4
sun

雲
wan4
cloud

雨
jyu5
rain

彩虹
coi2 hung4
rainbow

風
fung1
wind

雪
syut3
snow

行雷
haang4 leoi4
thunder

閃電
sim2 dim6
lightning

暴風雨
bou6 fung1 jyu5
storm

龍捲風
lung4 gyun2 fung1
tornado

霧
mou6
fog

冰雹
bing1 bok6
hailstones

大自然 NATURE
daai6 zi6 jin4

溫度 wan1 dou6　temperature

熱
jit6
hot

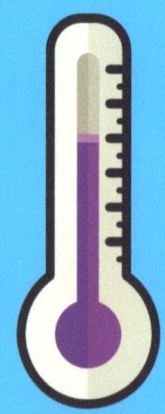
暖
nyun5
warm

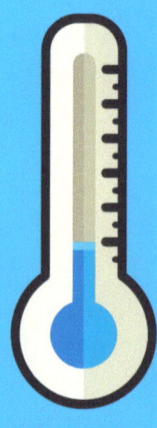
涼
loeng4
cool

凍
dung3
cold

天
tin1
sky

樹 tree
syu6

草
cou2
grass

花
faa1
flower

空氣
hung1 hei3
air

太陽
taai3 joeng4
sun

瀑布
buk6 bou3
waterfall

雲
wan4
cloud

山
saan1
mountain

水
seoi2
water

河 river
ho4

池塘 pond
ci4 tong4

太空人 taai3 hung1 jan4 Astronaut

水星 seoi2 sing1 Mercury

太陽 taai3 joeng4 Sun

火箭 fo2 zin3 Rocket

月亮 jyut6 loeng6 Moon

地球 dei6 kau4 Earth

火星 fo2 sing1 Mars

金星 gam1 sing1 Venus

木星 muk6 sing1 Jupiter

小行星 siu2 hang4 sing1 Asteroids

海王星 hoi2 wong4 sing1 Neptune

土星 tou2 sing1 Saturn

天王星 tin1 wong4 sing1 Uranus

冥王星 ming5 wong4 sing1 Pluto

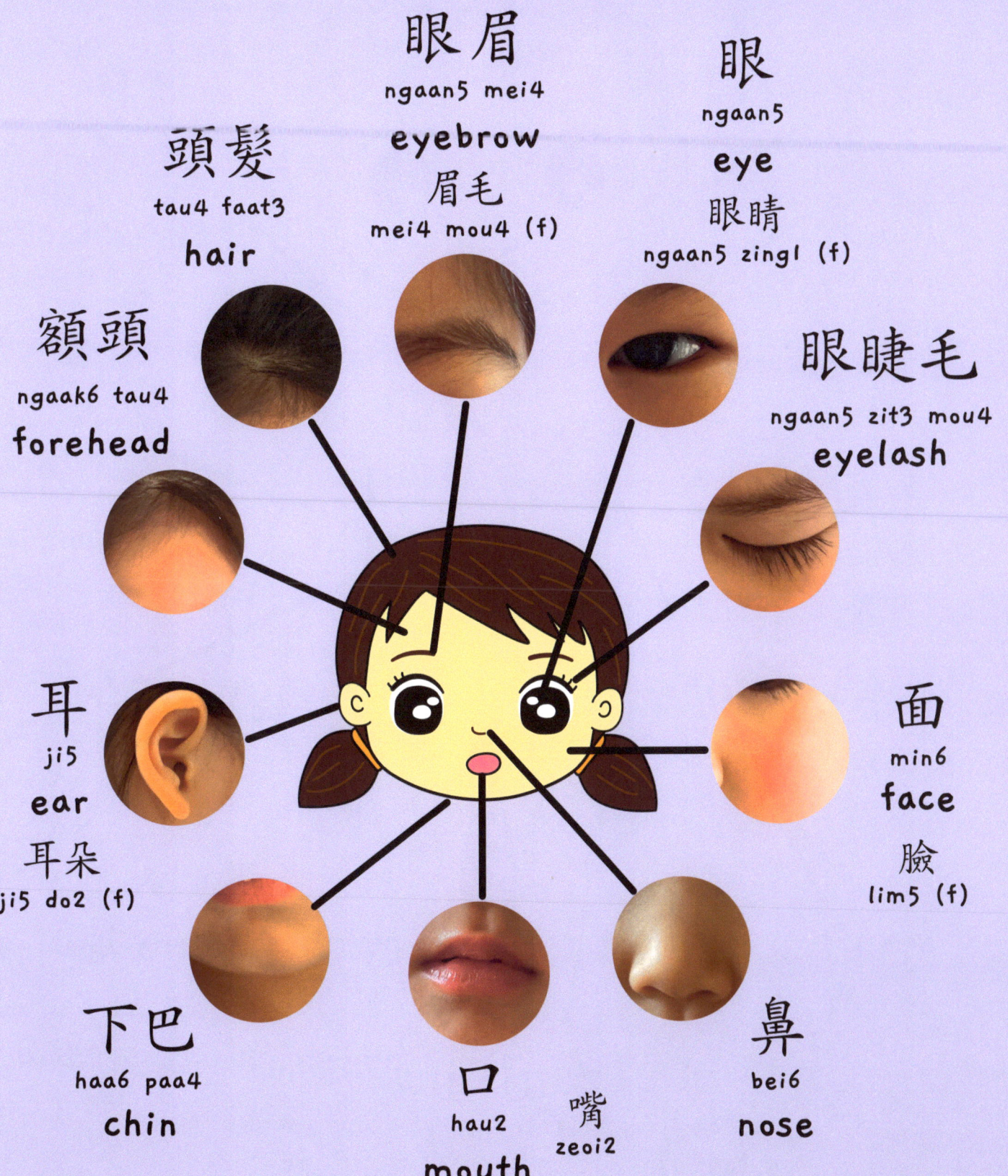

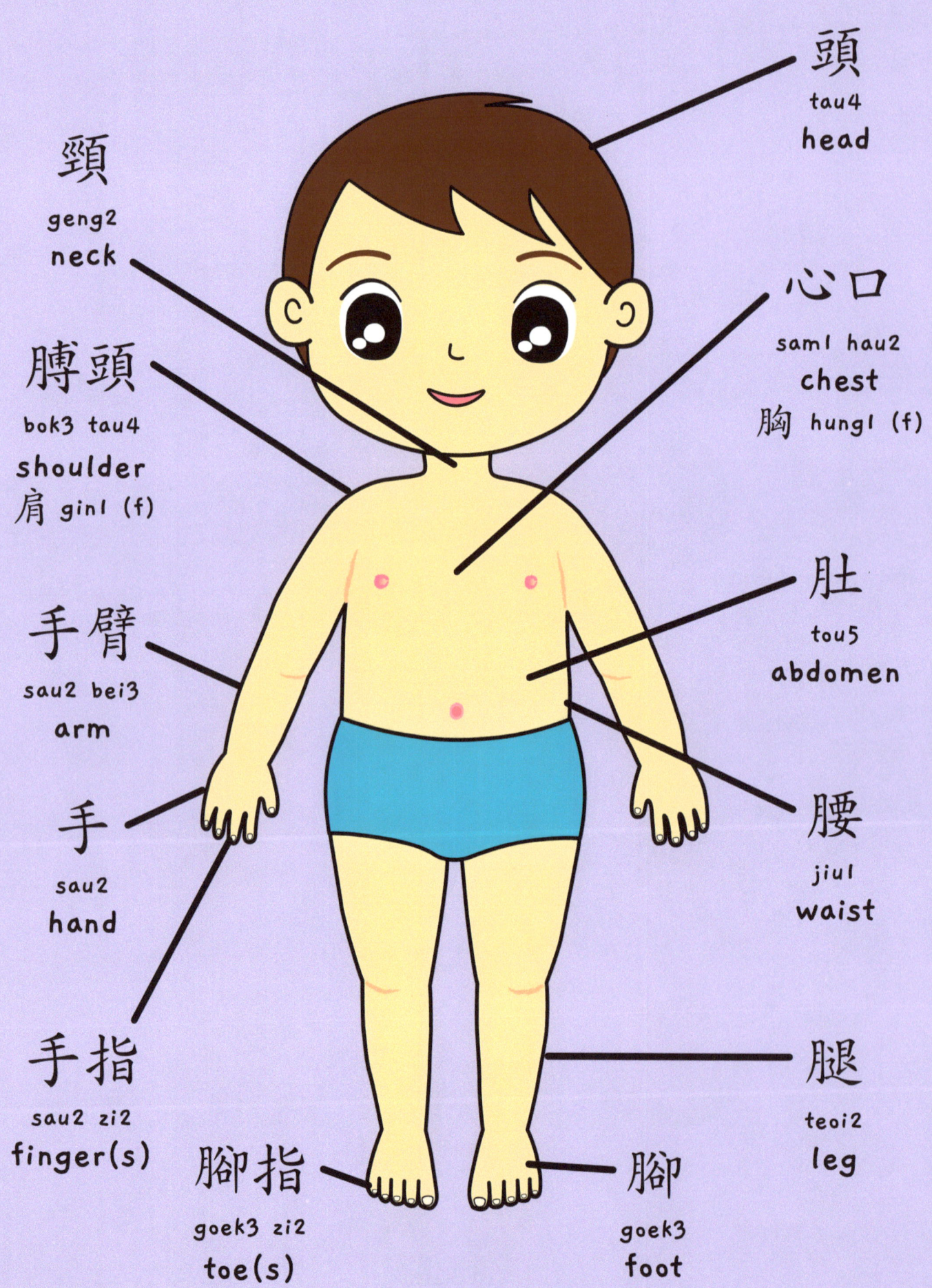

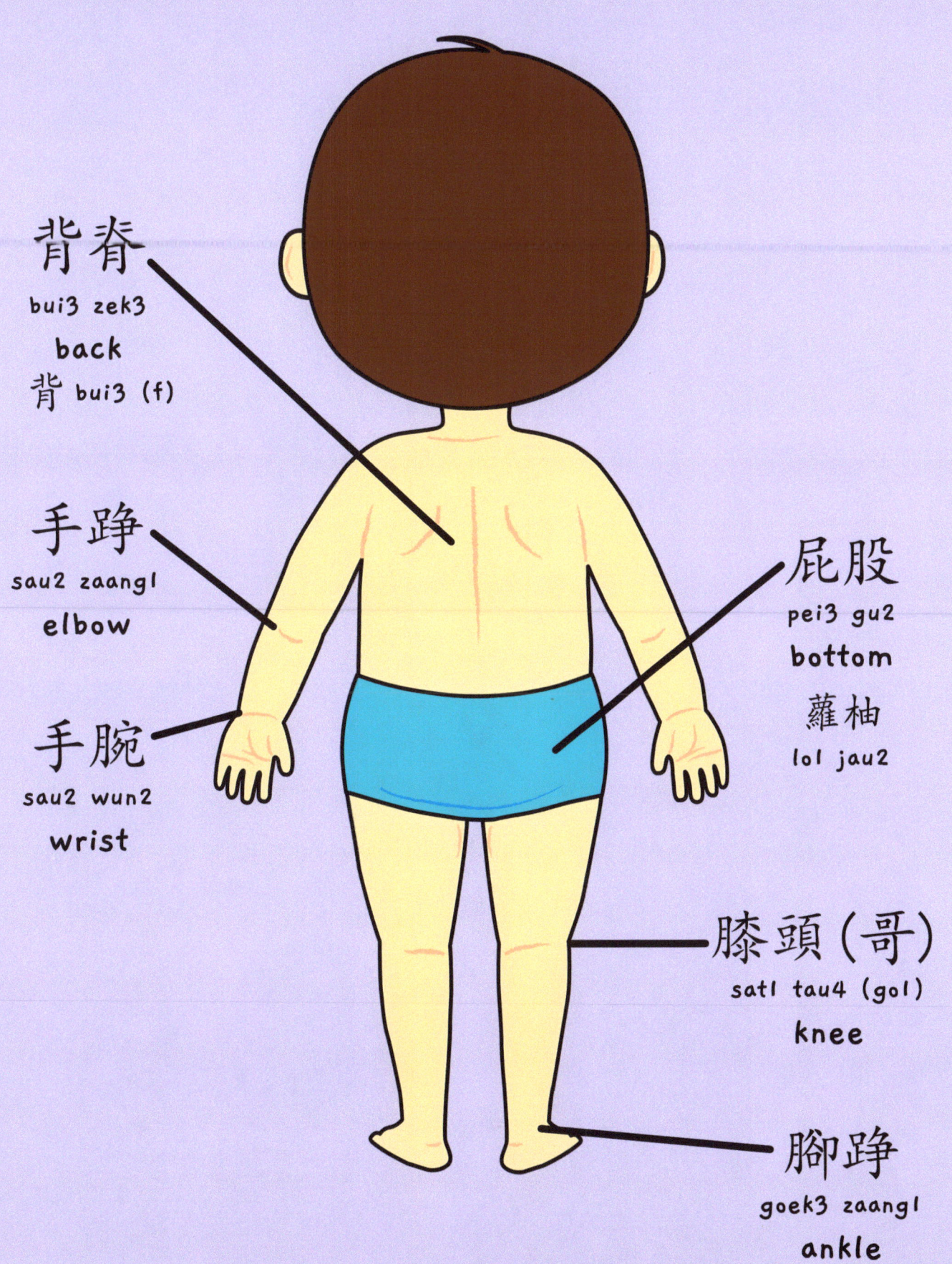

情感 FEELINGS
cing4 gam2

我覺得...　　　我感到...
ngo5 gok3 dak1...　ngo5 gam2 dou3...

I feel...

開心
hoi1 sam1
happy

滿足
mun5 zuk1
satisfied

傻
so4
silly

驕傲/自豪
giu1 ngou6 /zi6 hou4
proud

興奮
hing1 fan5
excited

平靜
ping4 zing6
calm

驚訝
ging1 ngaa6
surprised

悶
mun6
bored

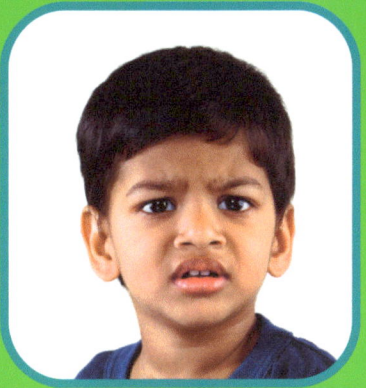
迷茫
mai4 mong4
confused/perplexed

緊張
gan2 zoeng1
nervous

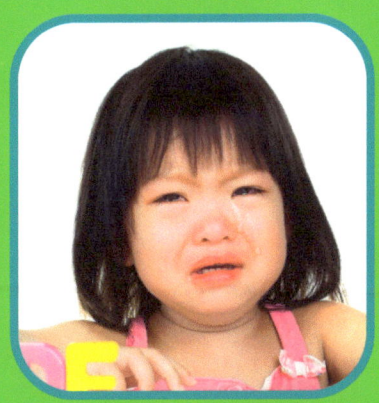
傷心/難過
soeng1 sam1 /naan4 gwo3
sad

嬲
nau1
angry

驚
geng1
scared

失望
sat1 mong6
disappointed

尷尬
gaam3 gaai3
embarrassed

29

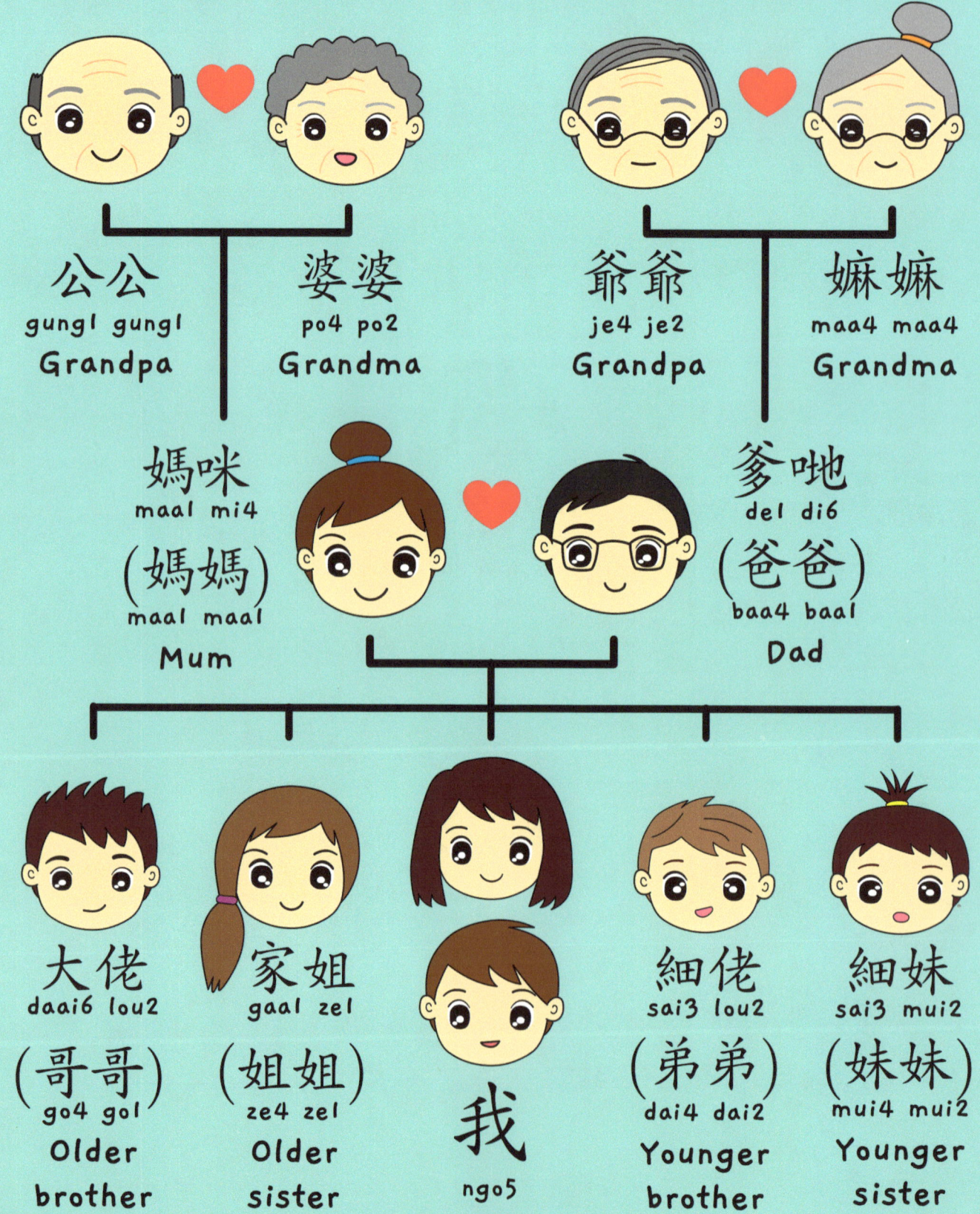

公公 gung1 gung1 Grandpa  婆婆 po4 po2 Grandma

OLDER THAN MUM | YOUNGER THAN MUM

舅父 kau5 fu2 Uncle (mum's older brother)

姨媽 ji4 maa1 Aunt (mum's older sister)

舅父 kau5 fu2 Uncle (mum's younger brother)

阿姨 aa3 ji1 Aunt (mum's younger sister)

舅母 kau5 mou5 Aunt

姨丈 ji4 zoeng2 Uncle

舅母 kau5 mou5 Aunt

姨丈 ji4 zoeng2 Uncle

All cousins are called...

表哥 biu2 go1 Older male cousin

表姐 biu2 ze2 Older female cousin

表弟 biu2 dai2 Younger male cousin

表妹 biu2 mui2 Younger female cousin

媽咪 maa1 mi4 / (媽媽) maa1 maa1 Mum

RED = relation through marriage

31

爺爺 je4 je2 Grandpa

OLDER THAN DAD

伯父 baak3 fu6 Uncle (dad's older brother)

伯娘 baak3 noeng4 Aunt

姑媽 gu1 maa1 Aunt (dad's older sister)

姑丈 gu1 zoeng2 Uncle

堂哥 tong4 go1 Older male cousin

堂姐 tong4 ze2 Older female cousin

表哥 biu2 go1 Older male cousin

表姐 biu2 ze2 Older female cousin

堂弟 tong4 dai2 Younger male cousin

堂妹 tong4 mui2 Younger female cousin

表弟 biu2 dai2 Younger male cousin

表妹 biu2 mui2 Younger female cousin

爹哋 de1 di6 / (爸爸) baa4 baa1 Dad

32

嫲嫲
maa4 maa4
Grandma

YOUNGER THAN DAD

阿叔/叔仔
aa3 suk1 /suk1 zai2
Uncle (dad's younger brother)

阿嬸
aa3 sam2
Aunt

姑姐
gu1 ze1
Aunt (dad's younger sister)

姑丈
gu1 zoeng2
Uncle

堂哥
tong4 go1
Older male cousin

堂姐
tong4 ze2
Older female cousin

表哥
biu2 go1
Older male cousin

表姐
biu2 ze2
Older female cousin

堂弟
tong4 dai2
Younger male cousin

堂妹
tong4 mui2
Younger female cousin

表弟
biu2 dai2
Younger male cousin

表妹
biu2 mui2
Younger female cousin

There are multiple variations of the tones used for relatives, so there is more than one right way for naming most relatives!

BLUE = cousins

33

動物 ANIMALS
dung6 mat6

狗
gau2
dog

貓
maau1
cat

兔
tou3
rabbit

雀仔
zoek3 zai2
bird

鳥 niu5 (f)

烏龜
wu1 gwai1
tortoise

青蛙
cing1 waa1
frog

牛
ngau4
cow

老鼠
lou5 syu2
mouse

馬
maa5
horse

公雞
gung1 gai1
rooster

母雞
mou5 gai1
hen

雞仔
gai1 zai2
chick(s)

小雞 siu2 gai1 (f)

35

羊 綿羊
joeng4 min4 joeng2 (f)
sheep

豬
zyu1
pig

驢
lou4
donkey

鴨
ngaap3
duck

昆蟲 INSECTS
kwan1 cung4

(媽)蟻
(maa5) ngai5
ant

甲蟲
gaap3 cung4
beetle

烏蠅
wu1 jing1
fly

蜜蜂
mat6 fung1
bee

毛毛蟲
mou4 mou4 cung4
caterpillar
also called 毛蟲 mou4 cung4

蝴蝶
wu4 dip2
butterfly

蜘蛛
zi1 zyu1
spider

also called
甲蟲
gaap3 cung4

瓢蟲
piu4 cung4
ladybird

蚊
man1
mosquito

海洋動物 OCEAN LIFE
hoi2 joeng4 dung6 mat6

海星
hoi2 sing1
starfish

魚
jyu2
fish

蟹
haai5
crab

海龜
hoi2 gwai1
sea turtle

章魚
zoeng1 jyu4 (f)

八爪魚
baat3 zaau2 jyu4
octopus

鯊魚
saa1 jyu2
shark

水母
seoi2 mou5
jellyfish

獅子魚
si1 zi2 jyu2
lionfish

龍蝦
lung4 haa1
lobster

海馬
hoi2 maa5
seahorse

海豚
hoi2 tyun4
dolphin

鯨魚
king4 jyu4
whale

車輛 VEHICLES
cel loeng2

車
cel
car

van仔
van zai2
van

小型貨車
siu2 jing4 fo3 cel (f)

電單車
din6 daan1 cel
motorcycle

綿羊仔
min4 joeng2 zai2
moped

also called 電單車
din6 daan1 cel

單車
daan1 cel
bicycle

滑板車
waat6 baan2 cel
scooter

滑板
waat6 baan2
skateboard

三輪車
saam1 leon4 cel
tricycle

消防車
siu1 fong4 ce1
fire engine

救火車
gau3 fo2 ce1

警車
ging2 ce1
police car

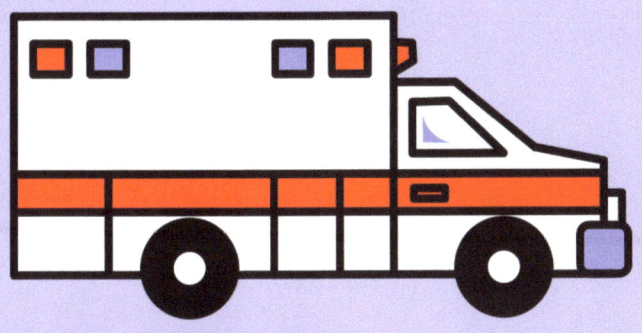

救傷車
gau3 soeng1 ce1
ambulance

救護車
gau3 wu6 ce1

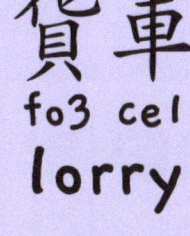

貨車
fo3 ce1
lorry

郵車
jau4 ce1
mail van

垃圾車
laap6 saap3 ce1
garbage truck

41

巴士
baa1 si2
bus

的士
dik1 si2
taxi

電車
din6 ce1
tram

火車
fo2 ce1
train

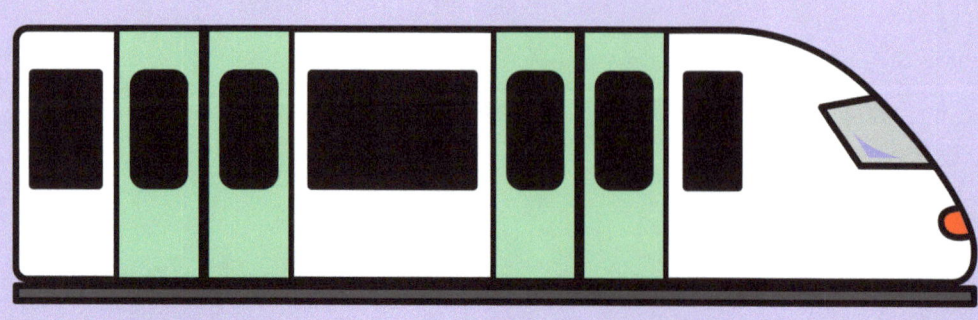

地鐵
dei6 tit3
metro
/subway

海空運輸
hoi2 hung1 wan6 syu1

SEA & AIR TRANSPORT

熱氣球
jit6 hei3 kau4
hot air balloon

飛機
fei1 gei1
aeroplane

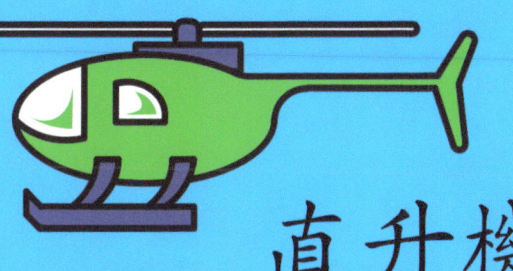

直升機
zik6 sing1 gei1
helicopter

船
syun4
ship/boat

帆船
faan4 syun4
sailboat

潛艇
cim4 teng5
submarine

水果   FRUIT
seoi2 gwo2

蘋果   香蕉   橙
ping4 gwo2   hoeng1 ziu1   caang2
apple   banana   orange

梨   雪梨   桃
lei2   syut3 lei4   tou4
pear   Asian pear   peach

黑莓   奇異果   藍莓
hak1 mui2   kei4 ji6 gwo2   laam4 mui2
blackberries   kiwi fruit   blueberries

菠蘿
bo1 lo4
pineapple

鳳梨
fung6 lei4 (f)

西瓜
sai1 gwaa1
watermelon

石榴
sek6 lau2
pomegranate

西柚
sai1 jau2
grapefruit

芒果
mong1 gwo2
mango

士多啤梨
si6 do1 be1 lei2
strawberries

提子
tai4 zi2
grapes

車厘子
ce1 lei4 zi2
cherries

草莓 cou2 mui2 (f)

葡萄 pou4 tou4 (f)
葡提子 pou4 tai4 zi2 (f)

櫻桃 jing1 tou4 (f)

蔬菜 VEGETABLES
sol coi3

青瓜
ceng1 gwaa1
cucumber

番茄
faan1 ke2
tomato

生菜
saang1 coi3
lettuce

洋蔥
joeng4 cung1
onion

菠菜
bo1 coi3
spinach

燈籠椒
dang1 lung4 ziu1
bell pepper

紅蘿蔔
hung4 lo4 baak6
carrot

西芹
sai1 kan2
celery

紅菜頭
hung4 coi3 tau4
beetroot

椰菜花
je4 coi3 faa1
cauliflower

薯仔
syu4 zai2
potato
馬鈴薯
maa5 ling4 syu4 (f)

牛油果
ngau4 jau4 gwo2
avocado

翠玉瓜
ceoi3 juk6 gwaa1
courgette
/zucchini

西蘭花
sai1 laan4 faa1
broccoli

辣椒
laat6 ziu1
chili pepper

蘑菇
mo4 gu1
mushroom

菜心
coi3 sam1
choi sum

食物 FOOD
sik6 mat6

拉麵
laai1 min6
ramen noodles

壽司
sau6 si1
sushi

烏冬麵
wu1 dung1 min6
udon noodles

炒飯
caau2 faan6
stir-fried rice

炒麵
caau2 min6
stir-fried noodles

咖哩飯
gaa3 lei1 faan6
curry rice

湯
tong1
soup

餃子
gaau2 zi2
dumplings

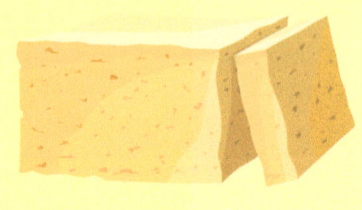
豆腐
dau6 fu6
tofu

48

奄列
am2 lit6
omelette
煎蛋卷
zin1 daan2 gyun2 (f)

披莎
pei1 saa1
pizza
意大利薄餅
ji3 daai6 lei6 bok6 beng2

意大利麵
ji3 daai6 lei6 min6
spaghetti
(abbreviated to
意麵 ji3 min6)

漢堡包
hon3 bou2 baau1
hamburger

薯條
syu4 tiu2
chips/fries

(墨西哥)捲餅
(mak6 sai1 go1) gyun2 beng2
(Mexican) burrito

沙律
saa1 leot2
salad

三文治
saam1 man4 zi6
sandwich
三明治 saam1 ming4 zi6

麵包
min6 baau1
bread

49

衣服 CLOTHES
ji1 fuk6

T裇
T seot1
T-shirt

冷衫
laang1 saam1
sweater/jumper

短褲
dyun2 fu3
shorts

(長)褲
(coeng4) fu3
trousers

短裙
dyun2 kwan4
skirt

(長)裙
(coeng4) kwan4
dress

褸
lau1
coat
外套 ngoi6 tou3

睡衣
seoi6 ji1
pajamas

底衫
dai2 saam1
vest

底褲　内褲
dai2 fu3　noi6 fu3
underpants

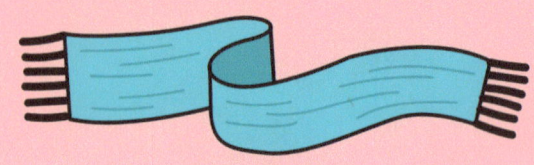
頸巾
geng2 gan1
scarf

襪
mat6
socks

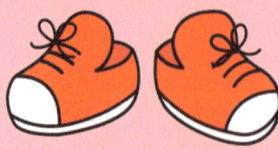
鞋
haai4
shoes

帽
mou2
hat

JYUTPING PRONUNCIATION

Cantonese is a tonal language that can be broken down into syllables. Each syllable can be a complete word in itself or can be combined with other syllables to create compound words. The same syllable can have a very different meaning based on the tonal inflection used. A classic example is the syllable 'maa'. When pronounced as maa1 with the 1st tone, it means 媽 i.e. mother. Alternatively, when it is pronounced maa5 with the 5th tone, it means 馬 i.e. horse!

Jyutping (粵拼), pronounced 'yoot ping', is a romanisation system developed in 1993 by the Linguistic Society of Hong Kong, and is one of the most popular romanisation systems to date. It is a representation of Cantonese sounds using the international phonetic alphabet. Jyutping breaks down each syllable into the initial sound, final sound and tone. For example, in maa5 (馬), 'm' is the initial sound, 'aa' is the final sound and the syllable is in the 5th tone.

There are six tones in Jyutping, represented by the number at the end of the syllable:

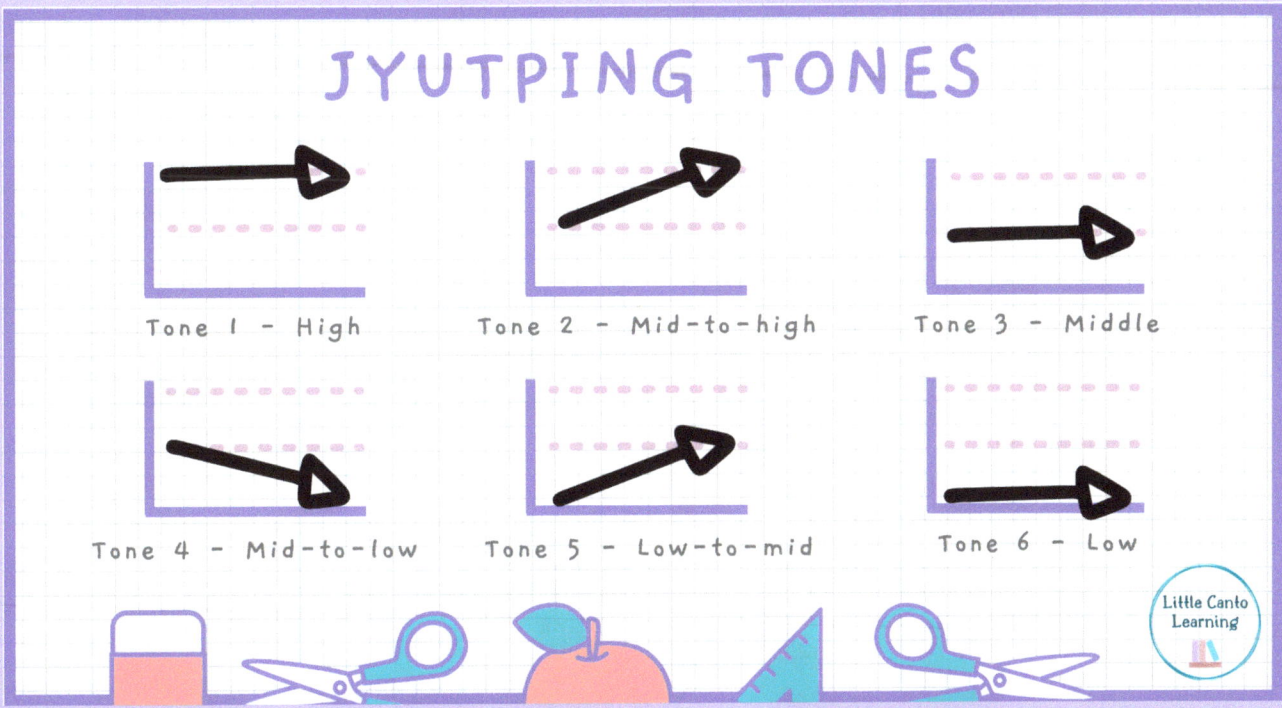

A pronunciation guide is beyond the scope of this book. However, there are lots of useful online resources covering Jyutping pronunciation in detail. These include lists of how the initial sounds, final sounds, and tones should be pronounced, with accompanying audio files.

There are some useful links at https://littlecantolearning.com/jyutping-pronunciation/

QR CODES

Scan the codes below with any QR code scanner to listen to audio pronunciations of the vocabulary.

Scan here to listen online
Password: HappyLearning2

Scan here to download
the vocabulary by chapter

Other books available:

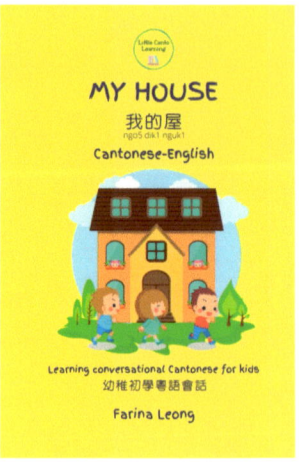

Thank you for purchasing this book!

If you found this book useful, a review would be much appreciated.